Never Mind

21 Day Devotional to being free

Kevin L. Nelson; MBA, MPA

Never Mind: 21 Day Devotional for
Being Free

Kevin L. Nelson

Published by Austin Brothers
Publishing, Fort Worth, Texas

www.abpbooks.com

ISBN 978-0-9996328-4-0

Printed in the United States of America
2018 -- First Edition

In memory of my loving mother
Robbie Lee Nelson
I honor you and the sacrifices you made to
give me a better life.

To my wife MaeEtta Nelson and my
daughter Kendall Nelson
you are the wind beneath my wings.

Patrick MaGrew
my mentor and Spiritual Dad
without you none of this would be possible.
Thank you for sowing and speaking life into
me and my family.

Day 1

The Gift of Being Alone

Jesus practiced solitude and silence. If He meditated how much more do we need to meditate?

"Very early in the morning while it was still dark, Jesus got up, left the house and went off to a solitary place, where he prayed." Mark 1:35

Often, the busyness of life gets us off track and we don't know if we are coming or going. Seldom, do most of us to make time to be alone and sit silently still.

There is great benefit to taking time and being silent. The stillness opens us up to hear what God really wants to say to our spirits.

Prayer: *Lord, thank you for this great gift. We know that it is in being alone that you can get our attention and do some of your best work to prepare us for what you have destined and called us to do and be.*

Never Mind

Psalms 46:10

Psalms 39:2-5

Mark 6:31-32

Matthew 17:1-2

Day 2

How Can I Win?

We can use the creative power of our words. What comes out of our mouths matters. We can prophesy our future to be good or bad. Proverbs 18:21 says, "Life and death are in the power of our tongue."

What are you saying on a daily basis about your family, future, and income? If you want to win in life, you must agree with what God says in His word.

We must learn to use our words to change situations we don't like. Don't use words to describe the situation. When you declare favor, abundance, and health you bless your life to win and not lose.

Don't speak negativity over your day. You need to send your words in the direction you want your life to go.

Prayer: *Lord, thank you I can win in life because you already promised the victory through you. I just have to remember to keep my eyes fixed on you.*

Deuteronomy 20:4

1 John 5:4

Proverbs 18:21

Day 3

When Talent Is Invisible

We all come to earth with a talent or multiple talents. Some people come to know very easy and early what their talents are but for others it can take a lot of time, effort, and energy.

This is something that we must all go to God about on a continual basis. This conversation is important, because this is the answer to why you have been created, and what your purpose is here on earth.

Prayer: *Lord, thank you for the gifts and talents you have placed me. Grant me the wisdom to recognize all that you have given to me and to know how to draw it out.*

Ephesians 2:10

Exodus 35:10

Never Mind

James 1:17

Day 4

I Roll with The King

Start every day off in faith. You must come to know that you can accomplish everything God has set-out for you to achieve on a daily basis.

Perspective is key. In order to live life on purpose and happy, we need to have a grateful spirit.

It's all about how we choose to see the situation in our lives. As believers we can know in our hearts that God is sovereign and strong.

We can and should believe that His plans for us are good, and that he has blessings in store as we follow Him.

Prayer: *Father God, because of you, I can face tomorrow or anything that may come my way because you live in me I know that you hold my future and that I can depend on you.*

2 Thessalonian 2:13

Day 5

When Ambition Is Low

We all have to deal with adversities at some point in our life. We frequently battle discouragement when our dreams don't come true on our timeline. It's good if you have family, friends, coaches, or teachers to cheer you on.

But, one thing I have learned is other people will not always be there to keep you encouraged. If we want to raise our ambition from being low, that encouragement has to come from the inside.

We must learn to encourage ourselves in the Lord. The Bible says "Hope thou in God." Psalms 42:5.

King David had to do that, he knew how to draw strength and encouragement from within.

There is a saying "that when you are down to nothing God is up to something."

Prayer: *Lord, help me believe in what you have called me to be when my ambition and dreams are too low, give me the strength and wisdom to dream higher for myself to complete the work I was born to do.*

1 Samuel 30:6

Day 6

The Conflict Within

The Bible says "It is with the mind that we serve the Lord" (Romans 7:25). When we feel as if we are losing our mind, it is due to not controlling the thoughts we allow.

We can find no solution when too many thoughts rush in and pile up on top of each other. We have the ability to control our thoughts, words, and actions. If we don't believe it, we will never do it.

The problems of life that come against us are opportunities to exercise the good things that God has given us. I will never develop self-control unless I am tempted to lose control.

God will never give us more to handle than we can handle calmly. If I am overloaded, it is my own fault. I have not managed my schedule well, I have put myself in a position where I have said yes to too many things.

Jesus has already provided His peace. All you have to do is receive it.

Prayer: *Lord, teach me how to deal with the conflict on the inside and to use all the weapons you have given me to be victorious in battle.*

John 14:27

2 Corinthians 5:7

Day 7

The Edge

Past mistakes can hold on to you long after they have occurred. Some of us hold onto things for years! We must begin to realize that the past. Sometimes, it's hard to wrap our head around the fact that we can't undo the past; it's over and done with.

What we have to do is create a redo button in our lives. You can meditate and write down how you would have done things differently if you could go back and do it again.

This helps us affirm that we have learned from our past mistakes and that we now have the skills to do things differently. Maya Angelou has a quote that states "when I know better I do better."

Prayer: *Lord, I want to live life on the edge, and be set free from the bondage of playing it safe after I have* *made a mistake. I know that I am the righteousness of God and that you have paid the price for my past, present, and future sins.*

Ecclesiastes 9:1-12

Day 8

Face to Face

As a believer in Jesus Christ, you must have an "and/or" faith. It means to believe God will deliver me and then... or God will deliver me or..., but either way my fidelity stays with Him.

It doesn't matter which option God chooses when I face the fire. God is either going to bring me out of it, or He's going to bring me through it, but what I'm not going to do is compromise the integrity to my relationship because of the threat.

Listen, the three Hebrew boys didn't know that the fire wasn't going to burn them up, they didn't care.

You have to get to a point in your life where you say, I don't care! For Him I live, for Him I die, for Him I get up, for Him I go down. Blessed be the name of the Lord! I don't care!

I'm talking right now to all of you who may be going through the fire. Sometimes you have to go through the fire and other times you walk around the fire.

I'm not coming out of it. I don't know when it's supposed to be over but until then I'm just walking, I'm just walking around in this problem until God steps in and deliver me.

Prayer: *Lord, when I come face to face with the storms of live, give me hope and strength in You, knowing that You have not left me but that You will come into my situation to walk with me through the fire.*

Daniel 3

Day 9

Never The Less

God will make a way for us to do everything He places in our hearts. He does not put dreams and visions in us to frustrate us.

God does not usually call people who are capable on their own; if He did, He would not get the glory. What gives God glory is when you go through hell and are at the bottom, and the Lord holds your life together. That's when I know He's real, and I must have a "never the less" attitude.

The Lord will sometimes let the worst happen, and what seems to be you hitting rock bottom and there is nothing else you can do, God will still wake you in the morning, He'll give you joy, and make ways out of no ways, so that people around you will wonder how in the world you are still managing. The only answer will be there must be a

God somewhere.

Prayer: *Father, I thank you for a "never the less" spirit you have given me everything I need for the life I am now living. Help me when I want to give up and give in. With you I can do all things.*

2 Thessalonian 3:13

Day 10

Attitude Is Everything

There is a saying that "attitude determines altitude." A persons attitude can help them get to where they may be trying to go or hinder them by keeping them going around the same mountain.

All of us have experienced the good, the bad, and the ugly, and our attitude can propel us into those places that will keep us down or raise us out of the pit.

When I think of the life of Joseph, he never showed himself to be down but continued to do good even when life was not making sense. The good thing about when God brought him out of all his trouble he never went back but finished his life as the prime minister of Egypt.

One's attitude can be the difference maker that will change your life and bring you to the mountain top over your problems.

Prayer: *Lord, I want to say thank you for the attitude you have given me. I ask that you would create in me a clean heart and give me an attitude adjustment to help me go higher in you.*

Philippians 4:8-9

Ephesians 4:4-6

Day 11

Let Nothing Offend You

How is that possible? Psalm 119:165 says that those who love the Word have great peace, and nothing offends them. One of the meanings of the Greek word for "love" is "attachment." Attach yourself to what God says, and you'll detach from the power of what others have done or said to you. That's what it means to love God's Word.

Being offended traps you. *Skandalon* (offense) is the trigger of a well-baited trap. When an animal touches the trigger of a snare, it snaps down on him and he is trapped. When you are offended, you are the one caught in the trap. By thinking and knowing this, it will empower you to stay out of the traps.

We let others control us when we pay attention to what they did to us. What God did FOR you is greater than what others have done TO you. Focus on what God has done for you.

Fully express your anger and hurt out loud to God. Tell Him how much it hurt. Forgive the offender (out loud to God) whether you feel anything or not; and ask Him to heal you.

Prayer: *I am free from being offended. I am free from the emotions of offense, bitterness, and the right to feel mad. I will not be trapped by those feelings. I love God's Word. I attach myself to what He said and did. I refuse to pay attention to the wrong done to me. I forgive and release those that have hurt me. I express my feelings to God, and I am healed, in Jesus' Name!*

Psalms 119:65

Day 12

God Feel's So Far Away

Separation between us and God is a myth. The devil wants us to believe it's to keep us powerless. We *were* separated from God through our sin (Isaiah 59:2), but Jesus *took away* the sin through His blood. Therefore, the moment we are born again, there is *no separation* anymore. We sometimes feel that He is far away, but He is not. He is here. He is there.

Christianity is not about us finding God. It is that Jesus came and found us, spilled His blood to cleanse us from all unrighteousness, took us into His arms, and breathed His Spirit into us. Now He lives in every person who has accepted Him as their Savior and Lord. Romans 8:11 tells us that the Spirit of God lives in us!

Jesus said in Matthew 28:20, "Lo, I am with you always; even to the end of the age." There is no way to misinterpret this verse. Jesus is with YOU always. That has to warm your heart and comfort you. We must decide to take Jesus at His word.

Prayer: *I am not separated from God in any way. He is an ever-present help in my time of trouble. His ever-presence brings me help! I recognize that He is already in me. That's what makes my faith work. God is not far off. He is right here, right now.*

Isaiah 59:2

Romans 8:11

Matthew 28:20

Day 13

My Emotions Are Running Wild

God created us to live with positive and healthy emotions. It's the negative ones that can harm our lives, our relationships, and our future. The idea that we are "victims" of our emotions because of our gender, our culture, our ethnicity, or our personality type, must be eliminated. We all have emotions but sometimes they have us!

If you think sad thoughts, you will become sad. If you think joyful and faith-filled thoughts, you will become happy. As a man thinks within, so is he. (Proverbs 23:7.)

As you control your thoughts, you will control your emotions. Then you will not feel the urge to control others! (Proverbs 16:31-32.)

You must believe that you are in control and that you have been given self-control.

Prayer: *I am not under the control of my emotions anymore. They are under my control. As I fill my mind with good thoughts, they will become good emotions. I can control my emotions by my thought life, and my thought life is surrendered to God's Word.*

Proverbs 23:7

Proverbs 16:31-32

Day 14

I Feel Trapped

We've all thought that at times, but it's a lie. There's always a way out of what you're in; or a way into what you've been kept out of. The devil would love for you to believe you are trapped, and that there's no way out of the situation you're experiencing. He wants you discouraged, immobilized, and paralyzed.

There's nothing you can't impact through prayer. Prayer gets you unstuck. It gets you moving again. Prayer is powerful. "And all things, whatsoever you shall *ask* in prayer, believing, *you shall receive*." (Matthew 21:22)

When it seemed like the three men in Daniel 3 were going to be burned in the fiery furnace, Jesus showed up! What was an impossible situation was made possible because Jesus was with them. And He is with you now!

"I am the way, the truth, and the life" (John 14:6). He is the way when there just seems to be no way. *He is your way* out of whatever situation you are in. Expect Him to make a way.

Prayer: *He is with me no matter what fire I'm facing. When I feel trapped, I will think about one step I can take that will move me toward healing, blessing, and God's will for my life, in Jesus' Name!*

Matthew 21:22

Daniel 3

John 14:6

Day 15

I Don't Have Enough

This is a mindset that says, "I don't have enough money, I don't have enough time, I don't have enough friends, I don't have enough education, etc." These thoughts build an invisible fence that keeps you from being able to move forward in life.

Our God calls Himself: El Shaddai, the God of more than enough. We have more than enough of God living inside of us (Romans 8:11).

In 1 Kings 17, there was more than enough for Elijah and the widow.

In Exodus 16, there was more than enough for the children of Israel every day. In John 6, there was more than enough bread left over after Jesus fed the 5000. In Mark 5, there was more than enough anointing to heal Jairus, the woman with the issue of blood, and all the people that were sitting nearby!

Patience is critical. Farmers understand there is seed, time, and harvest (Genesis 8:22). Don't forget that *time* is the connector between the seed and the harvest.

Prayer: *I always have enough, because Philippians 4:19 says, God shall supply all my needs, according to His riches. I always have enough, because my God is more than enough.*

Romans 8:11

1 Kings 17

Exodus 16

John 6

Mark 5

Day 16

My Past Is My Problem

You truly are a new creation—if you are in Christ (2 Corinthians 5:17). The old has passed away. Your past is over! All things, including your past, work for your GOOD! While your past is over, God can still make it work to your advantage. Believe that (Romans 8:28).

You are more than a conqueror. That means your past doesn't conquer you! You have conquered it, by being in Christ. You're the head and not the tail! See yourself that way, and your past loses its grip on you (Romans 8:37).

In Acts 28:5, Paul shook off a serpent from his hand. And you have the power to do so as well (Luke 10:19, Mark 16:18). Nothing can harm you anymore—not even your past mistakes or shortcomings. Shake it off by speaking to it!

Prayer: I am a new creation in Christ Jesus; and no matter how bad my past was, it's not only forgiven— it's washed away! I am more than a conqueror, and I will not be pushed around by memories or people from my past.

2 Corinthians 5:17

Romans 8:28

Romans 8:37

Acts 28:5

Luke 10:19

Mark 16:18

Day 17

Everybody Gets Blessed But Me

One of the things that make us most unhappy is when we compare ourselves to others and to what they have. When we compare, we despair.

God honors His Word above anything (Psalm 138:2). Cling to His Word, and you will get honored with it. Promotion, increase, and rewards will come.

Fix your eyes on Jesus. He is the source of all that you could ever want or need (Hebrews 12:2). Every good and perfect gift comes from above. (James 1:17).

The testimony of what Jesus has done for someone else is the prophecy that He can also do it for you (Revelation 19:10)!

Favor surrounds the righteous on every side (Psalm 5:12). And you are the righteousness of God, by merely being in Christ.

Prayer: God is my rewarder. I adopt His thinking regarding my life and situation. I fix my eyes on Him, and He finishes my faith. Favor surrounds me, promotion surrounds me, and God's rewards surround me like a shield, in Jesus' Name!

Psalms 138:2

Hebrews 12:2

James 1:17

Revelations 19:10

Psalm 5:12

Day 18

What Is Up With Me?

The constant awareness of "falling short" is where the devil and religion want to keep us. This keeps us defeated and hemmed in by shame, rather than liberated through our divine nature. 2 Peter 1:4 says, "Through His promises, we share in the divine nature of God and escape the corruption that is in the world through lust."

Dwell on what's right rather than what's wrong. Go through the Scripture regarding who you are in Christ; what is yours in Christ, and what you can do in Christ. It›s staggering. Flood your mind with this new way of thinking.

1 Corinthians 15:34 (Amp.) says, "Awaken to righteousness; and you will not sin." When God thinks of you, He thinks of a victorious, conquering, strong, powerful, wise, and holy son or daughter.

Prayer: *I am the righteousness of God, through the blood of Jesus. I stand in the presence of God without guilt, shame, inferiority or condemnation. I am a joint heir with Jesus. When God looks at me, He sees His blood. He thinks of me like a conquering, powerful and holy son or daughter. I will not think of myself as anything less or more than what God thinks of me in Jesus Name.*

2 Peter 1:4

1 Corinthians 15:34

Day 19

I Feel So Stressed All The Time

Stress is very powerful. It is a collection of thoughts or fears that bear down on your mind until they penetrate you and control your emotions, your health, and your relationships.

There is no place where you can go outside of the mercy and grace of God. The battle is already won. Jesus did it all. Your fight is simply to believe that. That's when stress leaves.

Uncertainty is a source of stress. Jesus had peace and even slept in the midst of a violent storm (Mark 4:35–39). How? Because He declared, "We are going to the other side." God's words create certainty and certainty eliminates stress!

Prayer: *I am free from the power of stress. I don't have to get rid of all my problems to get rid of stress. I have a table in the presence of my enemies. They have no power over me.*

Mark 4:35-39

Day 20

Life Is Scaring Me

When you look around at all the news and evil in the world—whether it's natural disasters, terror, rumors of wars, disease, depression, etc., it can be pretty scary.

There is a lot of fear in the world but, guess what, it does not have to control you and your family.

In Luke 10:19, Jesus said: "Behold I have given you authority... over all the power of the enemy." The devil doesn't push us around. We push him around! Whatever we bind on earth is bound in heaven. (Matthew 18:18). You're never afraid of what you have authority over. Therefore; we have to know our authority.

We must expect God to show up even in the dark. As you fill your mind with God's love toward you, fear leaves under any circumstance. (1 John 4:18–19, 1 John 3:1).

Prayer: *I receive the gift of peace, and therefore I am not troubled. I have power, love, and a sound mind. I have authority over the enemy. No evil or disaster can harm me. God is my deliverer. I expect God to show up in my life today, in Jesus' name.*

Luke 10:19

Matthew 18:18

John 4:18-19

1John 3:1

Day 21

The New Me

God is the potter, and we are the clay (Jeremiah 18:1-6). God is working on you to make you what He wants you to be. Trust the Artist to make a masterpiece. Be flexible and adaptable. See yourself as a good work in progress.

Philippians 1:6 says, "He who began a good work in you will complete it until the day of Jesus Christ." Don't prejudge what is your capacity or what is your potential. He's only just begun!

He never gives up on you. Jeremiah 18:4 says, "the clay was marred, so He made it again." He didn't discard it. He made it again. Thank God! He's re-making you!

Whatever flaws you have, they are not the final sentence. You are now being transformed into the very image of Jesus! (2 Corinthians 3:18)

Prayer: *I am unlimited in my ability to grow and change. God is the potter, and I am the clay. I am what God says I am. He began a good work in me, and He will finish it. He is making me into something GOOD. I am His workmanship—His work of art. He's good at this and has been doing it a long time! I am not in bondage to my weaknesses and former limitations. In the name of Jesus!*

Jeremiah 18: 1-6; 18:4

Philippians 1:6

2 Corinthians 3:18

www.ingramcontent.com/pod-product-compliance
Lightning Source LLC
Chambersburg PA
CBHW051049030426
42339CB00006B/264